Nailah & Nash
Take Paris

by Jawad Williams
Art by Shiela Alejandro

Hi everybody! My name is Nailah and this is my little brother Nash.
We are very lucky; we get to travel all over the world
because our dad plays professional basketball.

We would love to bring you along so you can
experience the different cultures with us.
Our first stop: Paris, France!

Driving through Paris, we came to this huge circle where lots of cars were driving around very fast. Nash and I thought they were racing. We told mom and dad that we should join the race.

Nash, as usual, yelled out, "go fast!" They explained to us that
we were driving around the Arc de Triomphe, a very famous monument
in Paris that would lead us to the Champs-Élysées [shahn zey-lee-zey],
a very busy street with lots of shops and restaurants.

Our next stop was the Eiffel Tower. Nash and I were amazed at how tall it was.

It made all the other buildings look really small.

We made a trip here twice, once during the day and again at night.

At night, the Eiffel Tower lit up with dancing lights like a Christmas tree.
It was definitely a sight to see.

13

Next, we went to dinner.

The food was different and our parents always want us to try new things.

I wanted chicken fingers and fries and Nash wanted a cheeseburger.

Dad ordered for everyone and it was not what we requested.

Nash yelled "a bug", and pointed at dad's plate.

Dad laughed and ate what we thought were bugs.

It was a plate of snails, but in France it's called escargot.

Mom wouldn't even try dad's food, but she did order shrimp

and french fries that were yummy.

For dessert, we had French macaroons of all flavors.

Dad made up for trying to feed us snails.

After a fun night we woke up to a great breakfast.

My brother and I ate all the croissants our little stomachs could handle.

They had plain croissants and even croissants filled with chocolate.

My favorite was the chocolate croissants and Nash liked the plain ones

because mom would spread jelly inside of his.

We washed down all of our French pastries with orange juice

and then went off on our next adventure.

Today our parents took us to the world's largest art museum called the Louvre. It had to really be the largest museum in the world because my brother and I were both tired from all the walking. Mom and Dad really wanted to see a painting that they read about in school. After making our way to the front of a large crowd, they finally got to see the painting of this lady. I think her name was Mona Lisa.

After walking for hours, mom and dad treated us to
pizza and crème brulee, a famous dessert in France.
The Creme brûlée was a perfect ending to a long day,
then off to bed we went.

Besides all the sightseeing, another thing we loved to do was go to our dad's basketball games. He is our favorite player and we like to wear jerseys with his number and our names on them. My mom always dresses really cute too. I like to tell her "ooooooh you fancy girl", she laughs every time. I know I can't play out there with my dad and his teammates, but Nash doesn't. Nash thinks he is the best player in the world now, and dad always tells him, "put in the work" and he also tells us both, "education comes first".

We had a lot of fun in Paris, France and made a lot of new friends. I wonder where we will go next... wherever we go, I hope you guys join us for our next adventure in a different country. See you later!

-Nailah and Nash

Nailah and Nash's
Travel Necessities

① toys to play with on plane.

② A Tablet to watch movies or play games. Make sure you have your headphones

③ Bring all your favourite snacks.

④ Pack a jacket, sometimes it gets cold on the plane.

⑤ A coloring book and crayons.

Made in the USA
Columbia, SC
28 September 2020

21476162R00015